Rebuilding the Body

John-Michael Seeber

✸ Smithsonian

Contributing Author

Heather Schultz, M.A.

Consultants

Dr. Katherine Ott
Curator, Division of Medicine and Science
National Museum of American History

Tamieka Grizzle, Ed.D.
K–5 STEM Lab Instructor
Harmony Leland Elementary School

Stephanie Anastasopoulos, M.Ed.
TOSA, STREAM Integration
Solana Beach School District

Publishing Credits

Rachelle Cracchiolo, M.S.Ed., *Publisher*
Conni Medina, M.A.Ed., *Managing Editor*
Diana Kenney, M.A.Ed., NBCT, *Series Developer*
Véronique Bos, *Creative Director*
June Kikuchi, *Content Director*
Robin Erickson, *Art Director*
Seth Rogers, *Editor*
Mindy Duits, *Senior Graphic Designer*
Smithsonian Science Education Center

Smithsonian

Teacher Created Materials

5301 Oceanus Drive
Huntington Beach, CA 92649-1030
www.tcmpub.com
ISBN 978-1-4938-6697-7
©2019 Teacher Created Materials, Inc.
Printed in China
Nordica.072018.CA21800844

Table of Contents

An Old Idea with New Technology

Five thousand years ago, a woman walked through a crowd. She stood out because she was two meters (six feet) tall, but that was not all. If you saw her face, you might think she had special powers. It seemed as though fire or a small sun was shining out of her left eye. She had the earliest **prosthetic** (prahs-THEH-tik) eye ever found, a round piece of tar covered with gold. **Prostheses** (pras-THEE-seez) are artificial body parts. Since ancient times, people have found ways to replace missing or damaged body parts. Carved wood replaced a missing leg. A hook was used to replace a lost hand. Today, scientists and engineers are building better prostheses. Researchers are finding new ways to send signals back and forth between the brain and a prosthesis. Today, you can peel fruit or write a letter with an artificial hand. Technology can help people get out of wheelchairs and climb mountains. People work hard to create all these things. They keep working to turn problems into solutions.

prosthetic eye

This illustration shows a woman from around 2850 BC with a prosthetic eye.

4

Scientists found a big toe on a mummy that was made of leather and wood.

A Helping Hand

The human hand is complex. Hands are strong enough to hold heavy weights and gentle enough to pick flowers. Hundreds of years ago, a person with a missing hand might have used a hook, if they could afford it. Early engineers ran into many problems when they tried to replace missing limbs.

Many different skills were used to solve these problems. Ambroise Paré (am-BWAHZ pah-RAY) was a barber and a surgeon in the French army in the 1530s. When soldiers injured their hands, arms, or legs, their wounds could become infected. Sometimes, Paré had to **amputate** the wounded limbs.

Paré started making artificial hands so he could help **amputees**. He wanted to make a hand that could hold things. He invented the first mechanical hand. He called it *Le Petit Lorrain*. It worked using metal gears and springs. A French captain wore it into battle. He said it helped him hold the reins of his horse. Paré also designed a prosthetic leg that could bend at the knee. People often call him the Father of Prosthetics.

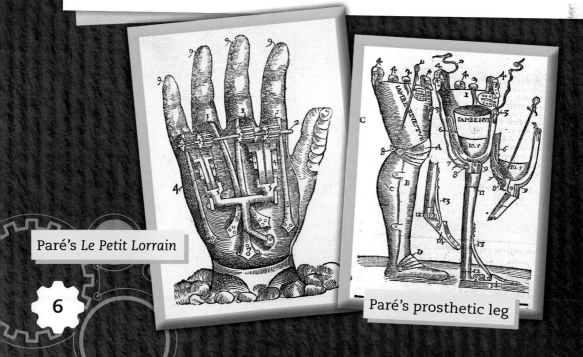

Paré's *Le Petit Lorrain*

Paré's prosthetic leg

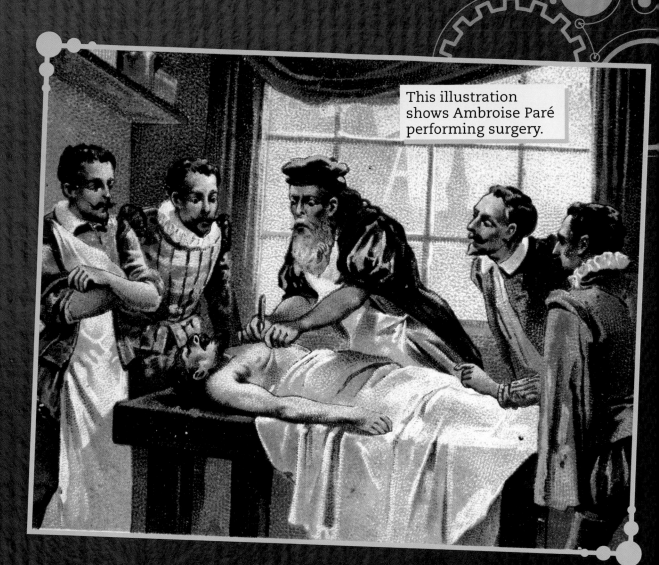

This illustration shows Ambroise Paré performing surgery.

TECHNOLOGY

Clamps Save Lives

In Paré's time, many people bled to death after amputation. Doctors did not have a good way to stop wounds from bleeding during surgery. Paré solved this problem by using a tool called a clamp. Clamps are still used in surgery. They pinch veins and arteries until doctors can sew them closed. Clamps keep many patients from dying during amputation.

Scientists want to make artificial limbs that do more of the things natural arms and hands can do. One problem is finding out how to make artificial limbs move.

Natural limbs move with just a thought. Cells called motor **neurons** send signals from the brain. These signals tell muscles what to do. Small hand movements use thousands of neurons. Moving a whole arm uses millions. Engineers are trying to control **bionics**, which are electrically powered prostheses, the same way.

The first step in moving bionics with the mind is to read brain signals. The second step is to find out how the new limb can read the signals. Engineers have developed a way to read some brain signals. They read motor neurons under the skin close to the missing limb. But this method cannot read many neurons at once. Some researchers are trying to get patients' brains to read signals directly from the spinal cord. This lets their brains read more neurons, but it is more dangerous.

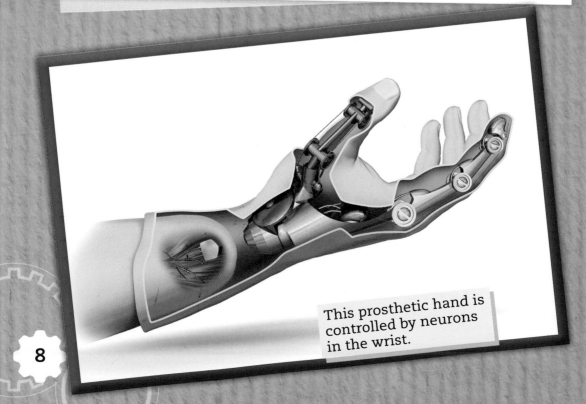

This prosthetic hand is controlled by neurons in the wrist.

This image shows one of the first fully functional bionic hands.

Some prostheses function but do not look like natural body parts.

This illustration shows how neurons connect muscles to the brain.

There are about 86 billion neurons in a human brain.

A Boy Wonder

Sometimes, boredom can lead to great ideas. Easton LaChappelle (luh-shuh-PEHL) was bored and looking for something to do. He decided to build a robotic arm. He was just 14 years old at the time. Because he didn't have many tools, he used LEGO® blocks and fishing line.

Living in a small town in Colorado, LaChappelle didn't have experts to help him. He found what he needed on the Internet. He had a friend who owned a **3-D printer**. This type of printer builds objects out of plastic. LaChappelle asked his friend to print better parts for the robotic arm. He entered the arm in the state science fair. At the science fair, he met a seven-year-old girl who had a prosthetic arm. The arm cost $80,000 and couldn't move in many directions. He decided to build an arm that she could use.

LaChappelle found a way to make less-expensive robotic arms, but there was still a problem. Most bionic arms require surgery to read nerves under the skin or to send neurons to different parts of the body. LaChappelle had to find a way to build a mind-controlled bionic arm that didn't require a risky surgery.

President Barack Obama shakes hands with the robotic arm created by LaChappelle.

3-D printed ear

3-D printed bone

Researchers have printed and implanted bone, an ear, and muscle structures. One day, they hope to print a human heart.

When LaChappelle was 16 years old, he bought a video game from the store. It had a headset that could read brainwaves. He wanted to use the toy to make his artificial hand move. So, he took the game apart and rewrote the software.

Not all of LaChappelle's ideas worked. He made a lot of mistakes. But he learned from those mistakes. He got his own 3-D printer so he could make parts quickly. If a part didn't work, he changed the design and printed a new one. He kept improving his design. After many tries, he finally built a hand that could be controlled with brainwaves. No surgery was required to make the artificial hand work.

LaChappelle built his bionic hand for under $500. He wanted other people to be able to build their own bionic hands. So, he put the instructions online. Anyone can download them for free. LaChappelle now runs a company that designs custom prostheses, and he still puts much of his work online for free.

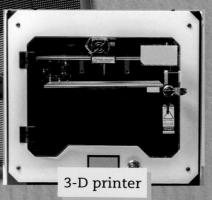

LaChappelle speaks at an event in 2017.

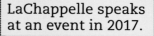

3-D printer

realistic prosthetic hand

ARTS

Making Machines Look Human

Parts made by a 3-D printer can look blocky. To make an arm that looks more lifelike, LaChappelle heated a chemical called acetone to 110° Celsius (230° Fahrenheit). At that temperature, it turned to **vapor**. He let the vapor cool on the blocky arm. It made the arm's surface smoother. After that, it was easier to slip a **silicone** skin over the arm to make it look more like a human arm.

Don't Walk, Run

For hundreds of years, artificial legs were made of wood. Then, scientists started making them out of lighter materials. But patients still complained that the legs were too stiff. This put stress on their backs and made it hard to walk. Artificial legs didn't move like human legs. Now, scientists are making bionic legs that help patients walk more easily.

Hugh Herr is a rock climber. He got frostbite on both of his legs during a mountain climbing trip when he was 17 years old. Both of his legs had to be amputated. But that didn't keep him down for long. Soon, Herr was climbing again on legs he had designed. They actually improved his climbing because he used rubber feet. After that, Herr studied engineering and the physics of how the body moves.

While he was learning, Herr was constantly trying new ideas. After building a device, he tried to make it better. He invented new artificial joints and ankles. Herr learned by trying again and again.

Hugh Herr

An athlete runs with a prosthesis shaped like a cat's leg.

ENGINEERING

Animal Inspiration

Some prostheses do not look like the human body at all. Instead, engineers look at nature to find a design that is even better. One type of prosthetic leg looks less like a human leg and more like a scooped blade. These legs were designed to work like the back legs of cats. They give runners a smoother running motion than other prostheses.

Herr realized that hardware alone was not enough. He needed to solve the problem of power. How do you replace the power people get from muscles?

He focused on the ankle. If he could invent an artificial ankle that could hold a leg up, it could help people walk. He created an ankle that had a spring and a battery in it. When a person put his or her foot on the ground, the spring wound up. When the foot lifted, the spring pushed the leg up. It helped move people forward with each step. Robotics had replaced the work that bones do. He called it the BiOM® ankle.

Walking was the first step, but people like to do other things, such as dance, carry heavy things, and hike up steep hills. Herr created software so the BiOM could work with the many ways people move their feet and legs. Because of his work, Herr can go hiking with his family, and many people can walk and run again.

Hugh Herr demonstrates BiOM.

Herr's ankle

Every Millimeter Counts

It used to be hard to get precise measurements to build prostheses that fit well. Now, computer scanners can quickly measure limbs to within a millimeter. A mathematical model is made from the measurements. This model shows stress points where pain is likely to occur. It also calculates how to fix them. The model is sent to a 3-D printer. The printer creates a prosthesis that is more comfortable.

A doctor scans an amputated limb.

Filtering Sounds

A lot of people can't hear well and need hearing aids to help them. But less than one-fourth of people with hearing problems actually use hearing aids. The reason is that most hearing aids don't do a very good job. Brains filter sounds that are not useful. This allows people to hear sounds that are important, such as voices. But hearing aids don't filter sounds, they **amplify** all sounds. Sometimes, background noises are louder than voices.

DeLiang Wang is a professor of computer science and engineering. When he was in college, his mother began to lose her hearing. Wang decided to fix the background noise problem. Scientists had worked on it before. But their devices filtered out too much sound. Patients still couldn't hear voices well.

Wang made a filter that separates voices from other noises. His computer program can tell whether a voice is louder or softer than background noise. Wang calls this **classification**. It helps the program learn patterns. This is similar to the way children learn to know the difference between speech and noise.

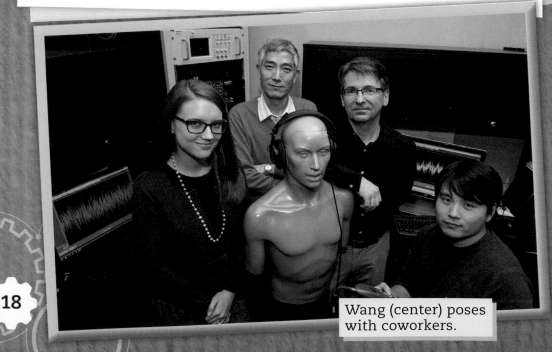

Wang (center) poses with coworkers.

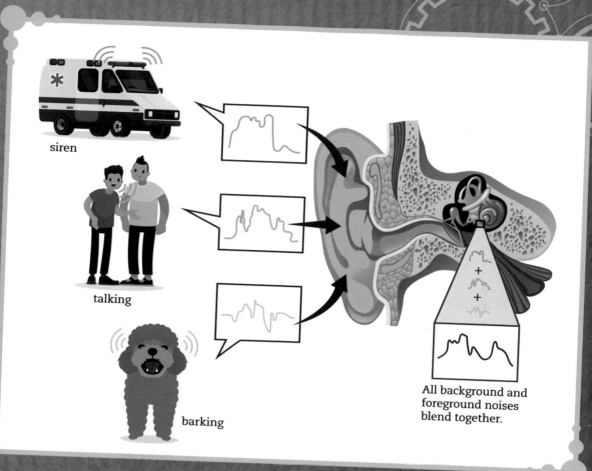

siren

talking

barking

All background and foreground noises blend together.

Waves of Hearing

Sound moves through the air in waves. Each wave has a frequency. Frequency is the number of waves that pass a fixed point in a certain amount of time. Imagine drawing a wavy line on a piece of paper. If you draw on top of it with a different colored pen, it is hard to tell the two colors apart. If we hear two sounds of the same frequency, we can only hear the loudest one. Identifying these frequencies is the first step in separating them for classification.

At first, Wang's filter worked in his lab but not in the real world. The real world is full of many different sounds. He made the program better by adding multiple layers. The results were good. People with hearing loss who used it had greatly improved hearing. Even people with normal hearing who used it heard sounds better. But there were still sounds that got in the way.

Wang decided the machine needed to learn more sounds. He is finding more sounds to add to the program. His team is using 10,000 sound effects from movies to help the program learn. He will keep looking for more and more sounds to fine-tune the program.

Once the program is ready, Wang wants to use it in an earpiece or smartphone. This could provide better hearing to millions of people. It could help people in loud factories or in the military. We may one day have a device that allows us to hear better than anyone has ever heard before!

A girl uses a hearing aid.

Hearing aids come in many sizes and shapes to fit all types of ears.

This device measures sound levels.

Digital Sound Level Meter

30   Fast   130

49.6

SPL   Range 30dB-130dB

MAX

LEVEL   A/C

FAST SLOW

An eardrum can burst if a sound is louder than 165 **decibels**. This is about as loud as a space shuttle when it launches.

Regaining Vision

Eyeballs are remarkable things. They send electric signals to our brains. Our brains turn the signals into images. That makes vision difficult to reproduce. The first step to copying vision is recording an image. The second—and hardest—step is sending that image to the brain. Scientists are working to solve this step.

One solution for people who have lost their vision is the Argus II. It's a device that records images and sends them to the brain. It comes with a pair of eyeglasses with a built-in video camera. A **microchip** is attached to the back of the eyeball and turns images into electrical signals. The microchip has 60 wires. These wires are called electrodes. They send signals to a part of the brain that passes them along to the **optic nerve**. This nerve connects the eyes to the brain. The brain then converts the electric signals into patterns of light for the person to see.

The surgery to attach the chip takes three hours. Patients can use the glasses after three weeks. The Argus II has already helped hundreds of people. But people could see more if there were more electrodes.

Argus II eyeglasses

Argus II microchip

This image shows a world as seen with normal vision (left) versus with Argus II glasses (right).

A man tests his vision after getting the Argus II implant.

VERS

The brain can identify an image that the eye sees in about 13 milliseconds.

23

How can more electrodes be added to the microchip? Scientists have worked on this problem for years. They are now building a special eye implant with diamonds. One diamond is carved into a box. The microchip is placed inside, and diamond electrodes are placed on top. These electrodes don't need wires. Without wires, there is room for many more electrodes. Scientists are trying to fit over a thousand electrodes on one chip. That would improve eyesight a lot.

Some diseases leave parts of eyes healthy, so they don't need a microchip. People might be able to see around the edges but not through the front of their eyes. Scientists are finding ways to use the healthy parts of these damaged eyes.

One way scientists do this is by putting tiny telescopes in damaged eyes. These telescopes are the size of peas. They send images to the healthy part of the eye. The patient learns to use the device to look ahead. The natural eye is used to seeing around the edges. More than six hundred people have had this surgery.

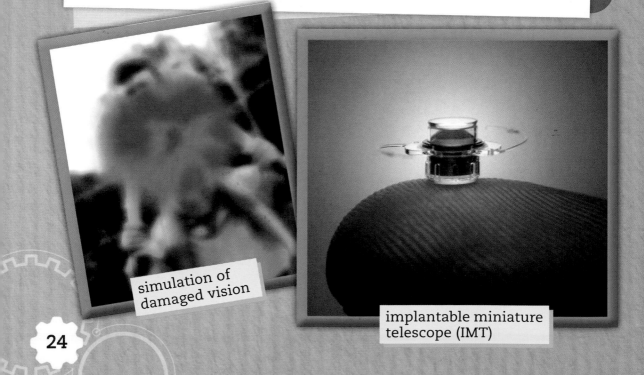

simulation of damaged vision

implantable miniature telescope (IMT)

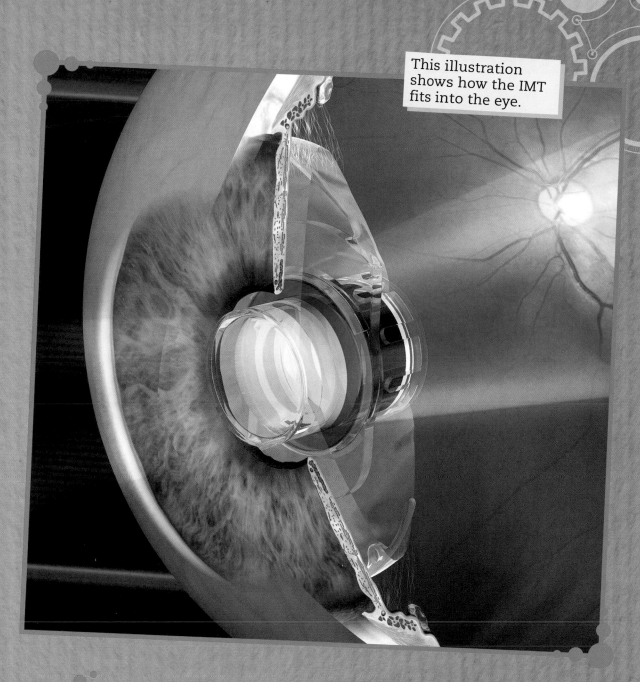

This illustration shows how the IMT fits into the eye.

Scientists are working on brain implants that will bypass the optic nerve to improve vision.

Superhero Powers

What do a barber, a teen, a mountain climber, and a professor have in common? Most people would say, "nothing." But Paré, LaChappelle, Herr, and Wang share a passion. They design and build devices. They help people who have lost the ability to use body parts.

These people find solutions to problems. During the process, they improve their designs. They spend years refining their devices over and over.

The desire to improve things makes a big difference. Just look at how far devices have come in the world of eye prostheses. They started with a ball of tar that was used in place of an eye. Now, diamonds and tiny telescopes are helping people see again.

What will be next? Researchers are already trying to go beyond what the average human can do.

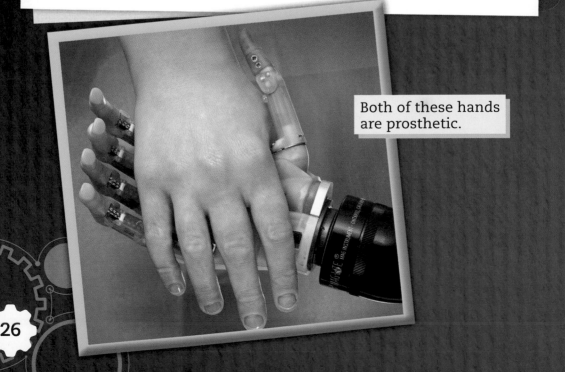

Both of these hands are prosthetic.

Engineers in Italy work on a suit that helps a person lift 50 kilograms (110 pounds) with each arm.

STEAM CHALLENGE

Define the Problem

Prostheses cannot just look like the part they are replacing; they must function like the part as well. Your task is to create a device that can pick up various objects and put them down like a real hand.

Constraints: Your device should be operated using only your thumb and index finger. It should be constructed with objects that are found around the classroom.

Criteria: Your device should be able to pick up the following items from a bucket: a number cube, an eraser, and a coin. Each object should be carried across the room and placed in an empty bucket without being dropped.

1 Research and Brainstorm

Look at all the ways your hand picks up objects. How can you replicate those movements in your device? What materials will you use to control your mechanical hand?

2 Design and Build

Sketch a plan for your device. Make sure to include which materials will be used for each part. Build your device.

3 Test and Improve

Use your device to lift one object out of a bucket and carry it across the room. Place the object in an empty bucket on the other side of the room. Repeat for each object in the bucket. If you drop an item, leave it on the floor where it fell. How did your device perform? Modify your design and try again.

4 Reflect and Share

How can you make your device more lifelike? Can your device be modified to move on its own? What changes would need to be made?

Glossary

3-D printer—a machine that prints three-dimensional objects

amplify—to increase strength or volume

amputate—to cut off a part of the body

amputees—people who have had body parts amputated

bionics—prostheses that are powered by electricity

classification—the process of grouping things based on ways they are alike

decibels—units for measuring how loud a sound is

microchip—a group of electronic circuits that work together in a very small space

neurons—cells that carry signals back and forth between the brain and the rest of the body

optic nerve—nerve from the back of the eye that connects to the brain

prostheses—artificial devices that replace body parts

prosthetic—describes a part of the body that has been replaced with an artificial device; describes the process of making an artificial body part

silicone—a water- and heat-resistant material

vapor—a substance that is in the form of a gas or that is made up of tiny drops mixed with the air

Index

Do you want to design prosthetics?
Here are some tips to get you started.

"Make some simple devices to use around the house, such as an extendable arm. Choose materials that work best in different situations. Then, apply that learning when you make other devices."—*Alexandra Lord, Chair and Curator, Division of Medicine and Science*

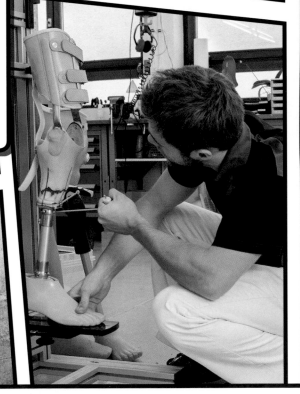

"I think of my job as understanding the history of the body and what makes bodies different. That includes topics like disability, race, and disease. These are all things that make us unique. There are a lot of things you can study to learn about the body. You can learn about biology, human anatomy, and even technology!" —*Dr. Katherine Ott, Museum Curator*